AWESOME MINECRAFT ACTIVITY BOOK

MC STEVE

UN UNOFFICIAL MINECRAFT BOOK

ENGINEERING

HOW TO PLAN A VILLAGE

There are plenty of pre-made villages in the Minecraft world, but visiting these villages isn't as fun as making your own. Of course, a village takes a lot of work, and it can be hard to know how to make your own village. Luckily, this activity book has the instructions you need! Follow these simple steps to make your own village.

1	Choose a biome to make your village in. • Superflat terrains will let you make most of your own landscape, which can either be fun or hard to work with. Other biomes will come with terrain, rivers, and plants, which can make other parts of making a village easier, especially if you are not playing on creative mode.
2	Find a mostly empty place (no forest) to build your village.
3	Flatten the village area. • It is difficult to build houses and other buildings on uneven ground. Making the village area flat will make building much easier.
4	Build roads, paths, and town boundary lines. • This will help you know where to put the buildings in your village, and it can help keep things organized.
5	Add buildings. • Add as many buildings as you want. This is your village, after all!
6	Add decorations. • Add the finishing touches once your buildings are done. Know that you can always go back and add more buildings later.
7	Add mobs. • Do you want chickens, squids, or other animals in your village? If so, add them now.

**PLAY THE GAME! ENJOY YOUR TOWN.
YOU PUT IN A LOT OF HARD WORK, NOW WALK AROUND AND HAVE FUN.**

THE TOWER JUMP CHALLENGE

Are you looking for something new to do in Minecraft? Well, look no further! The Tower Jump Challenge is a great game you can play by yourself or with friends. Here's how you play.

Find or make a body of water to jump into. It will need to be deep enough so if you land in it your character will not die. It does not have to be big, though.

You will need to be on creative mode to build the tower. You can either make a lot of towers, or you can add onto your tower after every jump. Make sure to place your tower next to your body of water. This tower should be a straight line going up into the sky. You can make it out of any material you want.

Now for the challenge. Fly your character up to the top of the tower. Once you are at the top, jump! Try to land in the water. If you make it, then you don't lose. Next, make the tower a little taller or make another taller tower and jump from there. Keep doing this until you miss the water.

You can take turns doing this with your friends to see who has the best aim, or you can practice by yourself. Try this next time you play Minecraft.

Good luck!

 # PLAN A GARDEN

Making a garden in Minecraft, and in real life, takes a lot of hard work and patience. If you have what it takes, then you will be able to make a wonderful garden that can give you all the food or flowers you want! All it really takes is some planning.

Follow these simple planning steps to make a basic garden. You can expand your garden later to make it bigger and better, and you can use these steps as often as you want, to make as many gardens as you want!

1	Decide where you want your garden to be. The last thing you want is to run out of room, so make sure you have enough space to build a garden, and maybe a fence around it. If you are not sure if the area you've picked is big enough, then just move to another spot.
2	Put down dirt blocks to plot your garden. The easiest garden pattern is to make a large square out of your dirt blocks. This will also make it easier to see where your garden is going to be.
3	Build a fence or border around your garden. This can make your garden look nice, and make it easier to see where your garden begins and ends. You can also put up decorations around your garden (but not inside) at this time.
4	Pick what plants to plant. Do you want a flower garden or a garden to grow food in? It's up to you, but decide now so your garden doesn't get messy later. Making a list of things you want can be helpful.
5	Put your tallest plants in the ground first. These are best put near the sides or the back of the garden so they do not get in the way of the other plants.
6	Put in your small plants. Make sure to leave some space for walking! Don't fill in the whole garden with plants.
7	Add paths or grass patches in your garden. You do not need to cover your whole garden in plants, but adding paths can make it easier to walk around, and adding grass makes it look nice, too.

That's all it takes to make a great garden! You can till the ground and harvest your plants easily with this set up! You can use this model every time you make a garden, if you want to. The possibilities are endless!

ORIGAMI TORCH

Origami is the ancient Japanese art of paper folding. It can be complicated at times, but below is a very simple outline for a Minecraft torch. All you need to do is color in the paper (the top square), cut it out along the outside lines, fold on the dotted lines, tuck in the tabs (gray areas) and tape it to keep it in place. The top square and horizontal row are the flames, and the rest is the stick. You can even use this pattern to make a bigger torch out of construction paper. Have fun!

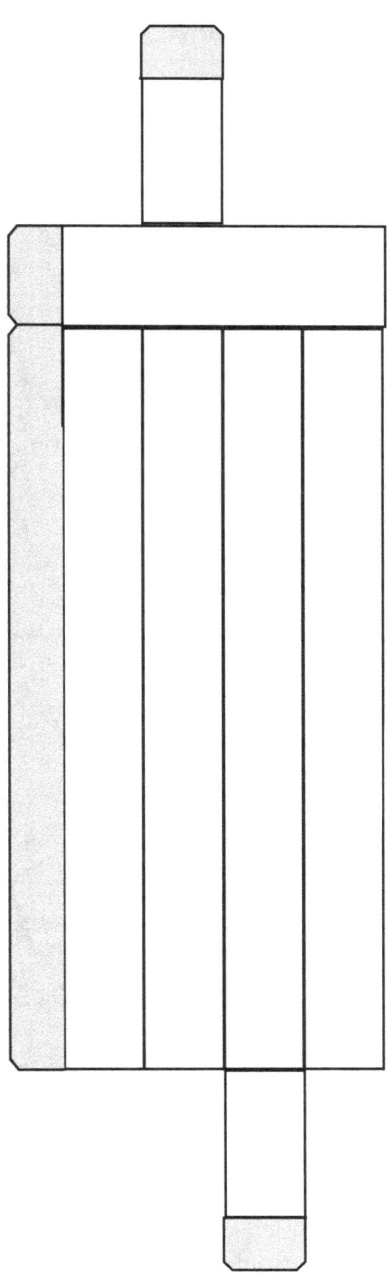

MAKE YOUR OWN HOUSE

Building a house in Minecraft is one of the best ways to keep your character safe from the mobs that like to walk around and cause trouble at night. Houses in Minecraft are usually made out of wood and stone, on the sides of mountains or in caves, or even underground. Most people who have played Minecraft before have built a house in the game, but have you ever tried building your own, real-life house in the game?

Building the house you live in outside of the game in Minecraft can be challenging, but it can also be fun. Below are some tips that might help you take on this challenge.

- *Playing this on creative mode will be the easiest way to do this, but it can be done on any mode you want.

- *Try building the walls of the rooms first. (If you live in an apartment, just do the rooms you live in, not the whole apartment building.)

- *Add the doors and windows once you have all the walls up.

- *Add carpeting, or change the colors of the walls to match the ones in your house.

- *Add furniture when you are almost done.

- *Add little decorations and details last.

HOW TO MAKE YOUR OWN RAILROAD

Making your own railroad can be easy and fun. All you need are some rails and a good imagination. The first step to making any good railroad is making the rails. All you need is some iron ingot and sticks. The recipe below will give you 16 railroad pieces. Do this as many times as you need to get all the pieces you need.

Iron Ingot		Iron Ingot
Iron Ingot	Stick	Iron Ingot
Iron Ingot		Iron Ingot

Once you have all the pieces you need, lay out the track to make it go wherever you want. Sadly, you will need to walk the whole way to place the tracks, but once your track is complete, you can use a minecart, instead.

If you come across hills, or if your minecart is running too slowly for your liking, you can add in some power rails to speed things up. However, it is important to know the speed they give doesn't last forever, and these rails cannot curve like normal rails can. They work best when placed on uphill slopes. This recipe makes six power rails.

Iron Ingot		Iron Ingot
Iron Ingot	Stick	Iron Ingot
Iron Ingot	Redstone	Iron Ingot

Once you make these and add them to your track, your railroad can take you just about anywhere. Put on a minecart, get inside, and zoom toward your next destination.

Have fun!

MAKE YOUR OWN BOARD GAME

Do you ever get bored? The next time you do, try to make your very own board game. You can do this in many different ways. A board and some suggestions are listed below for you to customize your game. Cut out this board, color it in, make up your own rules, and get to playing!

Game suggestions:

* Label the spaces with dollar amounts so people can "buy" the space they land on.

* Try to make it around the board once to win. Make a Start and Finish square.

* Add Spaces like "Roll again," "Skip a turn," and "Go back three spaces," to make the game more interesting.

ZOMBIE OBSTACLE COURSE

Zombies can be a menace in the Minecraft world, but they can be kind of funny to watch, too. One way to have some fun with zombies is to build an obstacle course for them. You can pit zombies against each other to see which one is the toughest, or you can play with friends to see which one of you can find the smartest zombie.

How do you make an obstacle course for zombies? However you want! However, there a few basic tips you should know.

* Zombies burn in daylight, so use your course at night or make sure you have enough shade to protect the zombies.

* High walls and fences will help keep the zombies inside the course.

* Putting a door or fence gate at the beginning of the course and closing it when the zombies begin the course can make sure they do not exit the course through the starting line.

Planning your course ahead of time can make it a lot easier to make, and you will be less likely to run into trouble with the course if you know what you are doing before you start building.

Below is a basic wall plan for an obstacle course. Inside this shape, try drawing different obstacles, like water, more walls, stairs, Creepers, or anything else that might make getting through the course tricky for zombies. When you are done, try building it in Minecraft to see if your zombies have what it takes to make it through.

Good luck!

FINISH THE PICTURE

Below is half of a famous mob from the Minecraft game. Your job is to draw the other half of the picture so it matches up with the half that is already drawn. This will take both artistic skill and planning. Take your time, and feel free to color in the picture when you are done!

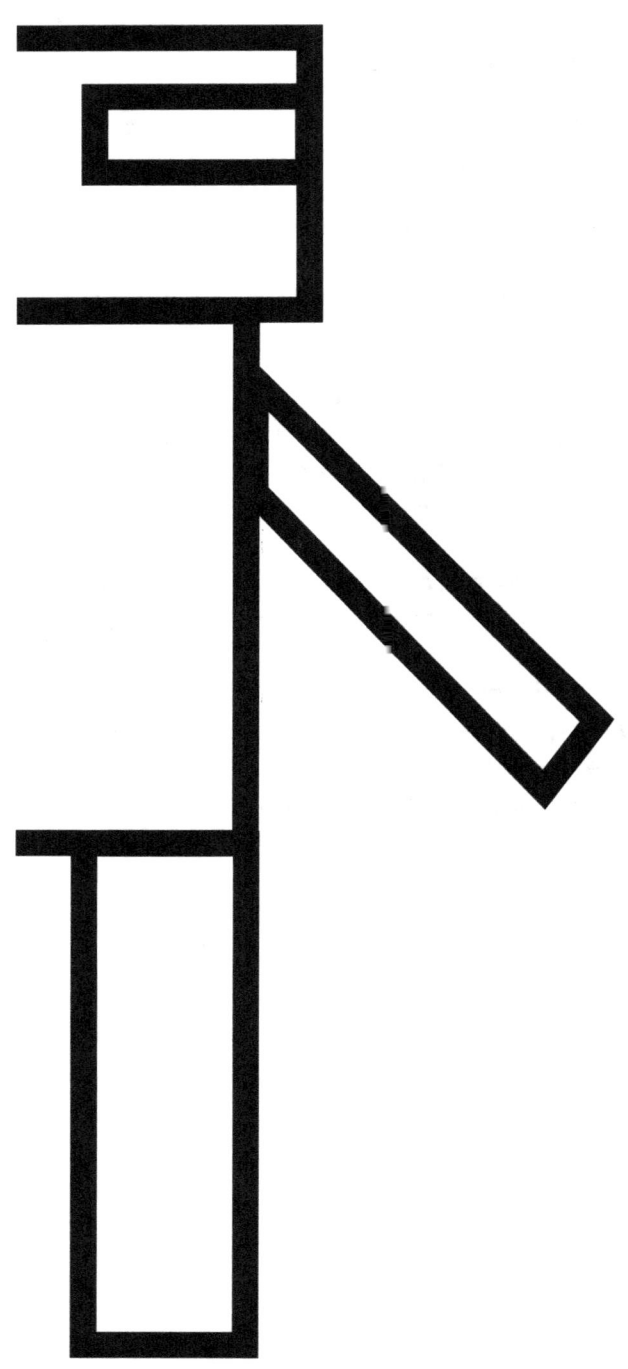

MAKE YOUR OWN WORDSEARCH

Making your own wordsearch can be fun and easy. You can make them for yourself to try after you have forgotten where the words are, or you can make them for your friends to solve. Since this is so easy, you can do this as many time as you want with different words!

Try using the squares below to make a wordsearch of your own! All you need to do is write in all the words you want to be found, and then fill in the rest of the spaces with random letters to hide the words.

For your first try, make a tool-based wordsearch. Try using these words in your puzzle, and feel free to add some more.

Tool, Shovel, Pickaxe, Bucket, Compass, Flint, Steel, Lead, Hoe, and Clock.

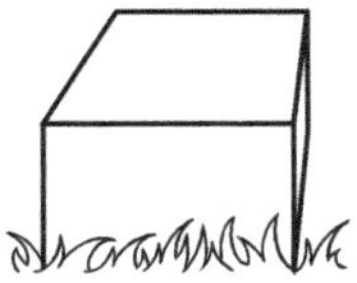

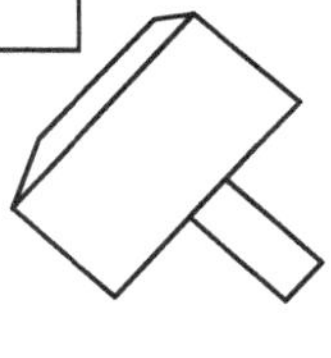

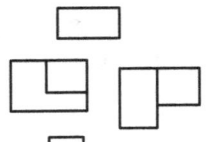 # MATCH THE TOOLS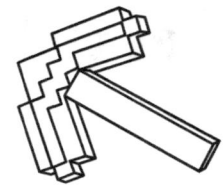

There are many useful tools in Minecraft, but do you know what all of them do? Try to match up each tool to what it does to complete this activity. Draw a line to connect the matching tool and action.

Tool	Action
Pickaxe	Shows what direction you are going
Shovel	Tells the time
Flint and Steel	Chops down trees
Shears	Helps catch fish
Hoe	Tills farm/garden plots
Fishing Rod	Cuts grass and other plants
Compass	Digs through soft materials easily
Bucket	Digs through tough materials easily
Clock	Helps start fires
Axe	Holds things like water and other liquids

WHICH MINECRAFT JOB IS FOR YOU?

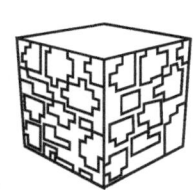

Have you ever wondered what your job would be if you were a character in Minecraft? Well, now you can find out. Take this personality quiz to find out which job you would be best at!

1. What do you like to do in Minecraft most often?
    a. Crafting
    b. Fighting
    c. Building
    d. Exploring

2. Which one of these mobs is your favorite?
    a. Iron Golem
    b. Herobrine
    c. Villager
    d. Creeper

3. Where is your favorite place to go in Minecraft?
    a. Forests
    b. The Nether
    c. Villages
    d. Everywhere

4. What would you do if you found an animal?
    a. Keep it as a pet
    b. Scare it away
    c. Eat it
    d. Leave it alone

5. Which of these things would you rather find?
    a. Potions
    b. Weapons
    c. Seeds
    d. Tools

Check your answers and use this chart to find the best job for you!

Mostly A's	Witch
Mostly B's	Monster Hunter
Mostly C's	Farmer
Mostly D's	Adventurer
A mix of all letters	Store Owner

MAKE A MINECRAFT PINATA

Every great birthday party has a pinata, and the best birthday parties are Minecraft themed! For this project, you may need help from a parent or guardian if you are very young. You do not need many things to make this creative pinata.

All you need to make your own pinata are these few things:

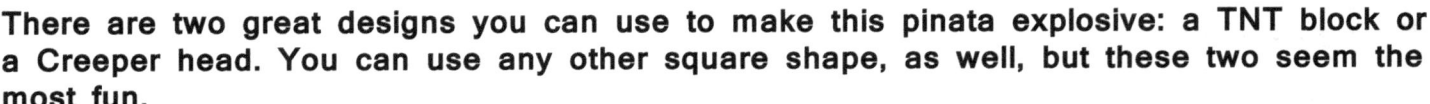

* Small or medium cardboard box
* Glue or tape
* Mache paper or construction paper
* Scissors
* Candy
* Markers

There are two great designs you can use to make this pinata explosive: a TNT block or a Creeper head. You can use any other square shape, as well, but these two seem the most fun.

Follow the instructions below to make your own pinata.

1. Build the box (if it is not built already) and cut three sides of a square on the top. This will work as a small hole to put candy in later.

2. Cover the whole box (except the hole) with construction paper or mache paper Glue or tape on the paper until it sticks. Red will make a great TNT block, and green will make a Creeper face.

3. Decorate the pinata!

    a. If making a TNT block, put a small white band around the middle of the box and glue it over the red paper. Write TNT in big black letters on each side of the box on the white strips.
    b. If making a Creeper face, just draw it on one side of the box if you used construction paper, or cut out black squares (out of construction paper) and glue it on one side of the box.

4. Fill it with candy! Square candies like butterscotch squares could make this fun Any candy will work, though.

5. Have fun! Break the pinata at your party and show off what you have made!

SILLY STORY

You will need a friend for this game. Tell them the word group in parentheses before the line, but don't read any of the other words to them until the story is done. You want it to be a surprise! Once they give you a word, write it on the line. When all the lines are filled in, read the silly story they have made back to them.

A Day at the Mine

(Person in room) _____ was ready for another day at the local mine. They had their trusty (tool) _____ in hand and they had packed a (adjective) _____ lunch to eat later in the day. Today was going to be a big day at the mine. Today, the workers would finally be mining for (block type) _____. Things were running smoothly enough, until (same person as before) _____ heard a (adjective) _____ noise coming from deep within the cave. They followed the noise, only to find (number) _____ (mob) _____ waiting for them. They didn't know what else to do, so they (verb) _____ toward the mobs. The mobs weren't scared, and they started getting angry. This made (person from before) _____ feel (feeling word) _____. They yelled, (exclamation) _____! Then they started to (verb) _____. This accidentally made an avalanche that crushed the mobs. They were free at last! They escaped the mine and treated themselves to a dessert of (food) _____. "What a tough day," they said. "I will feel (feeling word) _____ when I have to go back there tomorrow!"

17

MATH

COUNT BY...

Counting by ones is simple: 1, 2, 3, 4, 5...but can you count by other numbers? Count by the numbers below and fill in the blanks with the same pattern.

1. 2, 4, 6, ☐, 10, ☐, 14

2. 5, 10, ☐, 20, 25, ☐

3. 20, ☐, 40, 50, 60, ☐, 80

4. 3, 6, ☐, 12, ☐, 18

5. 4, ☐, 12, ☐, 20

6. 6, 12, ☐, 24, 30, ☐

7. 25, ☐, 75, ☐, 125

8. 100, 200, ☐, 400, ☐, 600

9. 1.5, 3, 4.5, ☐, 7.5, 9, ☐, 12

10. 1/2, 1, ☐, ☐, 5/2

FAMILY PHOTO

Steve invited his whole family to visit. Things were fun, but eventually, everyone had to go home. Before anyone left, they all took a picture together. In the picture there were...

2 moms, 2 dads, 2 grandparents, 6 kids, 4 grandkids, 2 sisters, 2 brothers, 3 sons, 3 daughters, 2 parents-in-law, and 1 daughter-in-law.

Based on the list above, can you guess the smallest number of people that could have been in the picture? Use the blank space below to do your math. This is tricky! Check your answer on the answer sheet to see if you got it right!

FARMING MATH BRAIN TEASERS

A local villager has a farm, and she has to do more math than she would like. She needs your help to solve these tricky math brain teasers. Try to see if you can crack these tough problems.

1 The farmer wants to build a barn. She needs it to be big enough for all of her animals. Her barn can fit four animals. She owns more than two animals. All of them are cows, except for two of them. All of them are horses, except for two. Lastly, all of them are pigs, except for two.

  a. Is her barn big enough for all her animals?

  b. How many animals does she have?

2 The farmer has a great harvest! She has 10 chests full of corn, and each chest has 10 pieces of corn inside. She decides to go to her neighbors' houses (she has 10 neighbors) and gives each of them one piece of corn.

  a. How much corn does she have left after she does this?

  b. Does she still need 10 chests to hold all her corn?

3 A neighbor asks how many chickens the farmer has. She tells him, "I just saw my chickens all lined up. There was one chicken in front of another, two behind the first one, and one chicken between the other ones."

  a. How many chickens does the farmer have?

FLOWER SHOP MATH

Sally the Villager owns a flower shop, and she has just gotten in some orders for beautiful flower bouquets. She needs your help to fulfill the orders. Solve these math problems to help Sally make her bouquets.

Sally has 10 blue flowers, and her friend wants to buy 5 of them. How many blue flowers will she have left after she sells 5 to her friend?

a.

Sally is running low on red flowers! She only has 2 left. Sally goes outside and picks 18 more red flowers. How many does she have now?

b.

Yellow flowers are popular today! Sally wants to make bouquets with 4 yellow flowers in each of them. She only has 20 yellow flowers, though. How many bouquets can she make?

c.

Sally's vases are the prettiest in town, and they are big, too. Each vase can fit 10 flowers. Sally has 3 vases left in her shop. How many flowers will it take to fill them up?

d.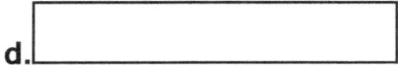

A customer comes into the store and wants 2 of every flower Sally has. Sally carries 6 types of flowers. How many flowers does she need to give her customer?

e.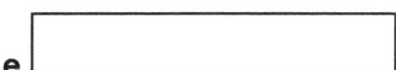

GUESS THE MOB

Below are some math problems that will give you hints that will describe a secret mob. These questions will test both your multiplication and division skills, as well as your knowledge about mobs. If you like this puzzle, you can even make your own like it to challenge your friends.

1. I have 4 x 5 health points if I am not attacked. How many health points do I have?

   a. [   ]

2. My attack strength is 7 x 7 if I am not charged. What is my attack strength?

   a. [   ]

3. I only spawn in areas with a 21 ÷ 3 light level or less. What light levels will I spawn in?

   a. [   ]

4. When a player defeats me, they earn 50 ÷ 10 experience points. How many experience points do they get?

   a. [   ]

5. I will become charged if I am hit with 9 ÷ 9 bolts of lightning. How many bolts of lightning do I need to be hit by to become charged?

   a. [   ]

6. Can you guess what mob I am?

   a. [   ]

HOW MANY BLOCKS...

Blocks are used to build just about everything in the world of Minecraft. That's why it is important to know how many blocks are needed to build things. These problems will help you test your skills, and may even help you build better when you next play the game.

1. You need to build a house that is ten blocks wide and five blocks long

    a. Not counting the floor, how many blocks will you need to make the outline of the house?

    [ ]

    b. How many blocks will you need to fill in the floor (not counting the walls this time)?

    [ ]

2. The house's walls also need to be seven blocks high.

    a. How many blocks will it take to fill up one wall on the long side of the house (not counting the blocks used to make the base of the house)?

    [ ]

    b. How many blocks will it take to fill up one wall on the wide side of the house (not counting the blocks used to make the base of the house)?

    [ ]

    c. How many blocks will it take to make all the walls in the house (not counting the blocks used to make the base of the house)?

    [ ]

When you are done with these tough questions, you can check your answers in the back of the book. You can even try to make this house in Minecraft (but make sure to add a roof and some doors!) and decorate it however you want, to have some fun as a reward for all your hard work! Plus, you'll know exactly how many blocks you need to build it!

Have fun!

MAKE FOUR

Solve the puzzles below. The answer to all of the questions is four. What you need to find out is how to get four by solving the problems below.
Good luck!

1 + ☐ = 4

2 x ☐ = 4

3 + ☐ = 4

4 x ☐ = 4

5 - ☐ = 4

6 - ☐ = 4

7 - ☐ = 4

8 ÷ ☐ = 4

9 - ☐ = 4

10 - ☐ = 4

MATH BRAIN TEASERS

Test your math and logic skills with these tricky math brain teasers. Check your answers in the back of the book when you are done to find out if you got them all right or not.

1. What weighs more? A pound of feathers or a pound of iron?

   a. [ ]

2. A Farmer has 10 sheep. All but five of them run away. How many sheep does he have?

   a. [ ]

3. What month has 28 days in it?

   a. [ ]

4. Steve has four apples and Alex takes three. How many apples does Alex have?

   a. [ ]

5. A farmer has two hens. One is a girl. What are the odds the other is also a girl?

   a. [ ]

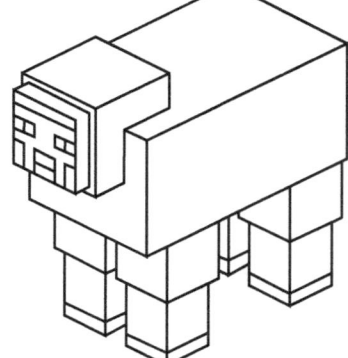

ALEX'S MESSAGE

Alex received a message, but it's all in numbers instead of letters! She has the codes she needs to solve the message, but she still needs your help to solve the math problems that are decoding the message.

Here is the code:

A	B	C	D	E	F	G	H	I	J	K	L	M
1	2	3	4	5	6	7	8	9	10	11	12	13
N	O	P	Q	R	S	T	U	V	W	X	Y	Z
14	15	16	17	18	19	20	21	22	23	24	25	26

Use this key to read the message below. Each word takes up one of the numbered questions below.

Example: 8.5.12.12.15 = Hello

Sentece 1	Sentece 2	Sentece 3	Sentece 4	Sentece 5
1. 20.15 2. 1.12.5.24	1. 20.15 2. 1.13 3. 3.15.13.9.14.7 4. 20.15 5. 22.9.19.9.20 6. 24.15.21 7. 6.15.18 8. 24.15.21.18 9. 2.9.18.20.8.4.1.15	1. 9 2. 23.9.12.12 3. 2.18.9.14.7 4. 3.1.11.5	1. 9 2. 8.15.16.5 3. 25.15.21 4. 12.9.11.5 5. 9.20	1. 6.18.15.13 2. 19.20.5.22.5

LOOK ON THE ANSWER SHEET TO SEE IF YOU SOLVED THE MESSAGE!

MINERAL MATH

Crafting is one of the most important things to do in Minecraft. Sometimes it can be hard to know if you have enough materials to make something, though. Solve these problems to see how great your math and Minecraft building skills are!

1. It takes 4 snowballs to make one snow block. You need 3 snow blocks to make a snowman in your yard. How many snowballs will you need to make 3 snow blocks?

   a. [   ]

2. It takes 9 diamonds to make 1 diamond block. You already have 6 diamonds. How many more do you need to make 1 diamond block?

   a. [   ]

3. It takes 5 leather to make one helmet. You have 10 leather. How many helmets can you make?

   a. [   ]

4. It takes 8 gold blocks and 1 apple to make 1 golden apple. You have 3 apples, but only 20 gold blocks. Do you have enough to make 3 golden apples? If not, why?

   a. [   ]
   b. [   ]

5. Last one! It takes 9 gold nuggets to make 1 gold ingot. You have 20 gold nuggets. How many gold ingots can you make? How many gold nuggets will be left over?

   a. [   ]
   b. [   ]

THE NAME GAME

Crafting is one of the most important things to do in Minecraft. Sometimes it can be hard to know if you have enough materials to make something, though. Solve these problems to see how great your math and Minecraft building skills are!

Name / Mob	Even	Odd
Steve		
Alex		
Blaze		
Creeper		
Enderman		
Ghast		
Iron Golem		
Villager		
Zombie		
Snow Golem		

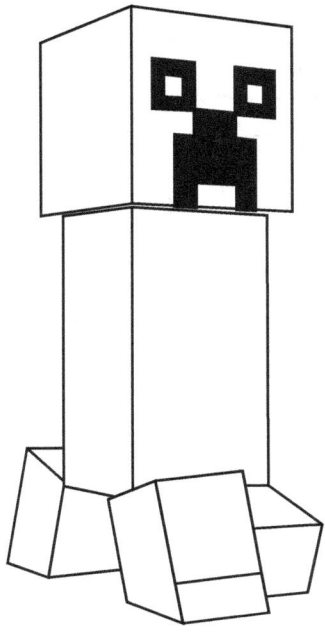

PIGS IN A PEN

Farmer Joe has three pigs that he needs to put into pens. However, these pigs need some space to move around so they don't feel crowded. There are nine spots in farmer Joe's pig pen, but the pigs can't be in the same row or column as another pig. It is fine for them to be diagonal, though.

There are six possible ways this can be done. Try to find out all the ways. Mark the spots where the pigs will go on the graphs below. When you are done, check the answer sheet to see if you got all the spots right!

30

SQUARE NUMBERS IN MATH

In Minecraft, nearly everything is made out of cubes and squares, but did you know that squaring numbers is an important thing to learn how to do in math? If you have learned about square numbers in school, then this can be great practice. If you haven't learned yet, then this project can help you get ahead of your class. All you need to do is know how to multiply numbers.

A square number is just one number times itself. For example, M x M would be M^2 but it wouldn't be 2M. An example with numbers could be 5 x 5 = 25.

Try your hand at the problems below to find what each number is when it is squared.

1. 1 x 1 =

2. 2 x 2 =

3. 3 x 3 =

4. 4 x 4 =

5. 5 x 5 =

6. 6 x 6 =

7. 7 x 7 =

8. 8 x 8 =

9. 9 x 9 =

10. 10 x 10 =

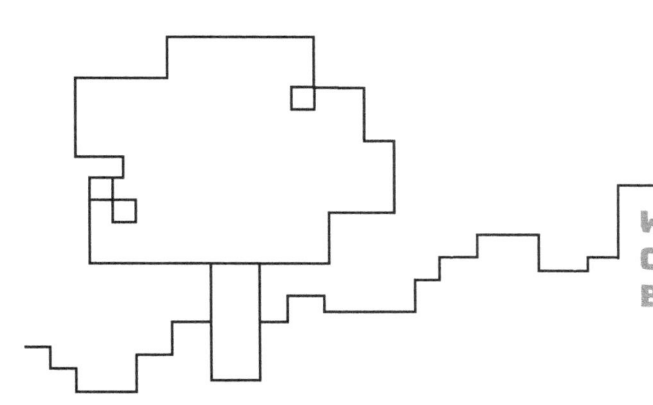

WHEN YOU ARE DONE SOLVING THE PROBLEMS, YOU CAN CHECK YOUR ANSWERS IN THE BACK OF THE BOOK OR WITH A CALCULATOR.

STEVE'S ODD PARTY

Steve is throwing a special "odd" party. He wants everything at the party to be in odd numbers to stick with his theme. Help Steve set up his party by helping him pick out the odd numbered things he needs to keep this theme as odd as possible.

1. To keep an odd number of guests, how many people should Steve invite?

    a. 10

    b. 15

    c. 20

    d. 18

2. How many balloons should he have?

    a. 25

    b. 36

    c. 10

    d. 50

3. How many pizzas should he bake?

    a. 2

    b. 3

    c. 4

    d. 6

4. How many pieces of candy should be in each goody bag?

    a. 11

    b. 22

    c. 44

    d. 66

5. Only one of Steve's friends has an odd number of letters in her name. She will be the guest of honor. Can you guess who she is?

    a. Alex

    b. Hannah

    c. Josie

    d. Kelsey

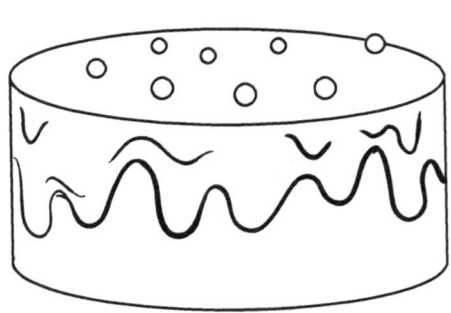

SUDOKU PUZZLE

Sudoku puzzles can be challenging, and fun! They are usually used with numbers, but they can also be used with letters and symbols.

Instructions: There are nine large squares, nine rows and nine columns. Each row, column, and large square can only have one of each number in them. If there is more than one of the same number in each of these boxes, then you will need to erase and try again. Try to solve the puzzle below!

	1	4	7	6		2		5
5			4	1			3	6
6	3	7		5	9	8	1	
	9				6		4	
2	5	6		7	4	9	5	3
4		1	9	3	5	6		
	4	2		8		3	5	
9		5	3		2	1	6	8
3	6		5	9	1		7	

TELLING TIME

Telling time in real life can be tricky, and so can telling time in Minecraft. The best way to learn how to tell time is to practice. Below are some practice time telling problems for you. If it will help, you can look at a clock or draw a picture of one to help you to solve these problems.

1. One day in Minecraft is ten minutes of real life time. One night is also ten minutes. How many minutes would it take to play through a whole day and night?

    a. ☐

2. How many Minecraft days and nights can you play through in one hour (60 minutes) of real life time?

    a. ☐

3. You are playing Minecraft at 7:00pm. Your parents say you can play for an hour and a half. At what time do you need to stop playing?

    a. ☐

4. How many Minecraft days and nights would you have played through during that time, assuming that you started on a new day?

    a. ☐ Days
    b. ☐ Nights

5. Two friends come over, but you only have two controllers. You have two hours to play the game, but you only get to play for 2/3 of the time (80 minutes). How many days and nights will you get to play?

    a. ☐

MINECRAFT DICE GAME

In this activity book, there are instructions to make your very own Minecraft dice. Now, here is an activity you can use them with. You will need at least two dice to play this game, but you can add more if you want to make the game a little more challenging. You can practice playing this game by yourself, but you will need another person to play it for real.

Here's how the game works.

1. One player will roll two (or more) dice.

2. All of the players will race to solve the addition problem made by both dice.

    a. For example, if you rolled a 5 and a 6, the players would need to figure out what 5+6 equals to win. The first person to get the right answer gets a point.

3. Keep playing the game until someone gets ten points.

    a. You can pick a higher number of points if you want, but ten is a good starting point.

If you want to make this game a little more challenging, you can add more dice to make the players add more numbers together, or you can try to multiply the two numbers on the dice instead of adding them.

THIS IS A GREAT WAY TO PRACTICE MATH BY YOURSELF OR TO CHALLENGE YOUR FRIENDS' MATH SKILLS. TRY THIS GAME TODAY TO SEE IF YOU HAVE WHAT IT TAKES TO WIN!

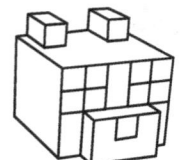 # TANGRAM OCELOT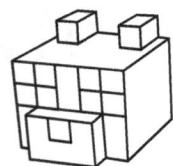

Below are some shapes you can cut out. Once you cut out these shapes, you must put them together to make the shape of an ocelot. Some of the shapes might overlap a little, but that's okay. The answer is in the back of the book on the answer pages.

When you are done, the cat should look like this.

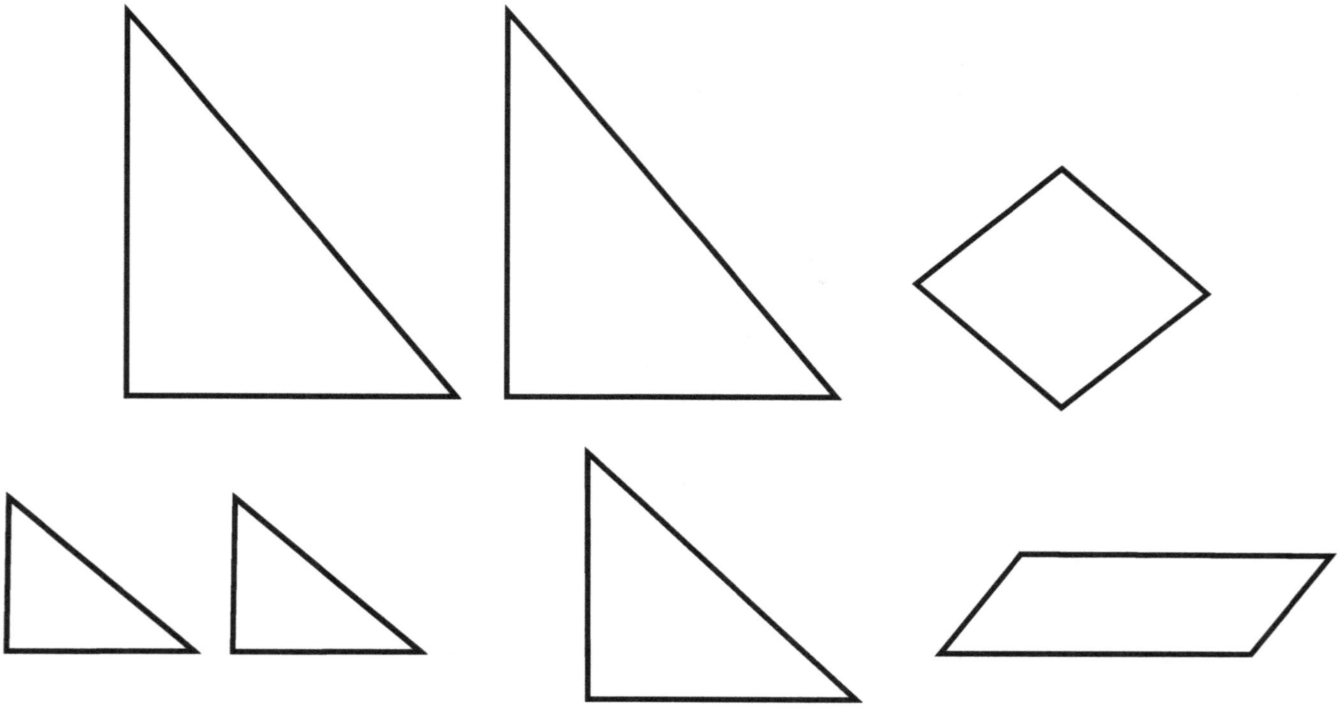

HOW TO DRAW 3D SHAPES

Drawing 3D shapes can be tricky, but luckily, this activity book has a handy guide for you. Once you learn how to draw 3D shapes well, you can draw your Minecraft creations on paper and make them look like they do in the game, instead of looking flat.

The first step when drawing a 3D shape is to start out with the 2D shape it comes from.

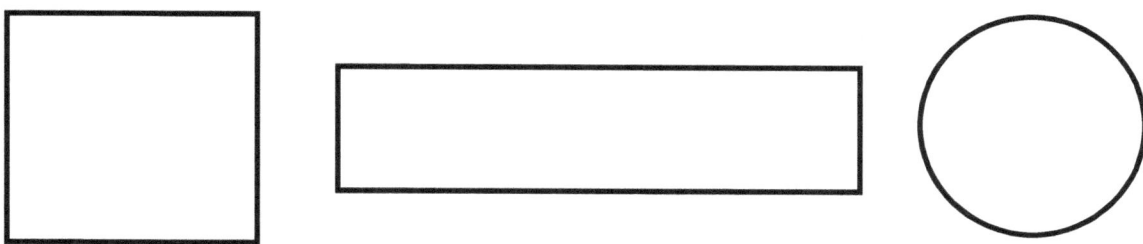

Once you do this, draw lines going out from each point. If you are working with shapes with no straight lines, then squish the shape and draw lines going down.

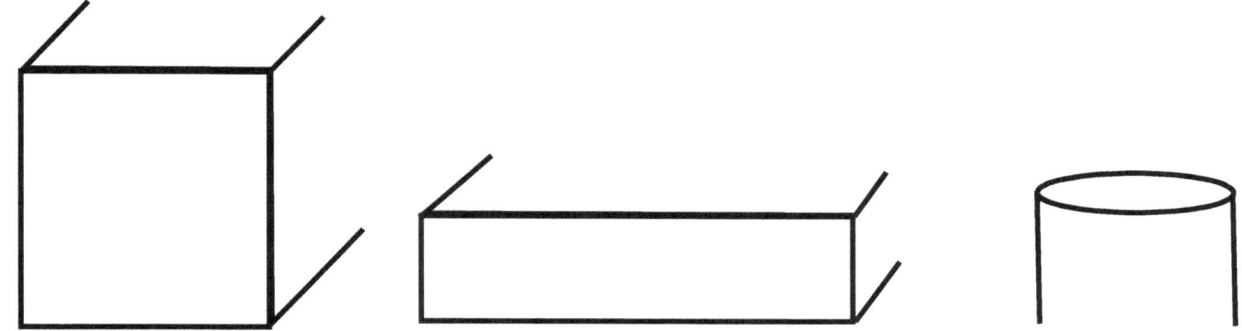

Once you do that, just connect the lines. You can even add shading if you want, to make it look even more 3D. You can use this guide with other shapes, as well.

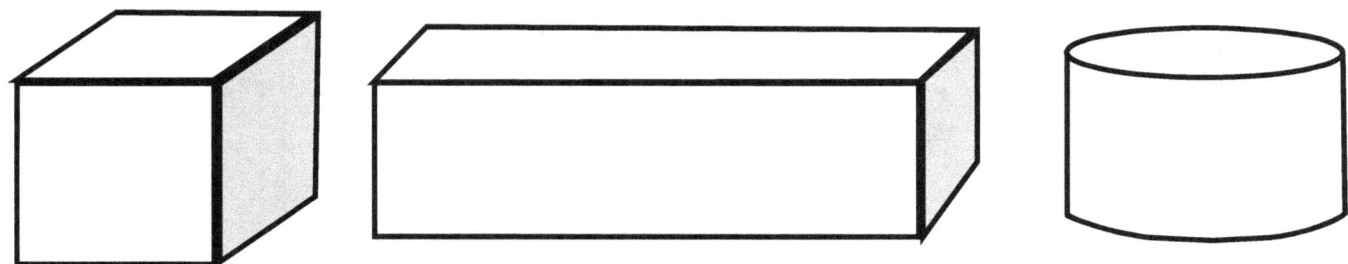

PRACTICE DRAWING THESE SHAPES AND OTHERS ON A SEPARATE PIECE OF PAPER TO SEE HOW WELL YOU CAN DO.

GOOD LUCK!

24

24 is the name of the game, and also the goal. Below is a chart full of the numbers 1 through 10. To play the game, just drop something small, like coins, onto the number chart. Use the three numbers your three coins (or other small objects) land on to try making the number 24. If you cannot make 24 with the numbers, then throw your items on the chart again to get new numbers. You can use addition, subtraction, multiplication, and division to get to this goal.

Example: Say you get the numbers, 3, 1, and 8. You could do 3 x 1 = 3. Then 3 x 8 = 24.

1	2	3	4	5
6	7	8	9	10
1	2	3	4	5
6	7	8	9	10
1	2	3	4	5
6	7	8	9	10

FRACTIONS COLORING MYSTERY

Below is a hidden picture that can only be revealed if you solve the fractions in each square. Color each square according to its matching fraction to see the picture. When it's done, you should see a well-known Minecraft monster!

BLACK = 1/2   GREEN = 1/4   BLUE = 1/3

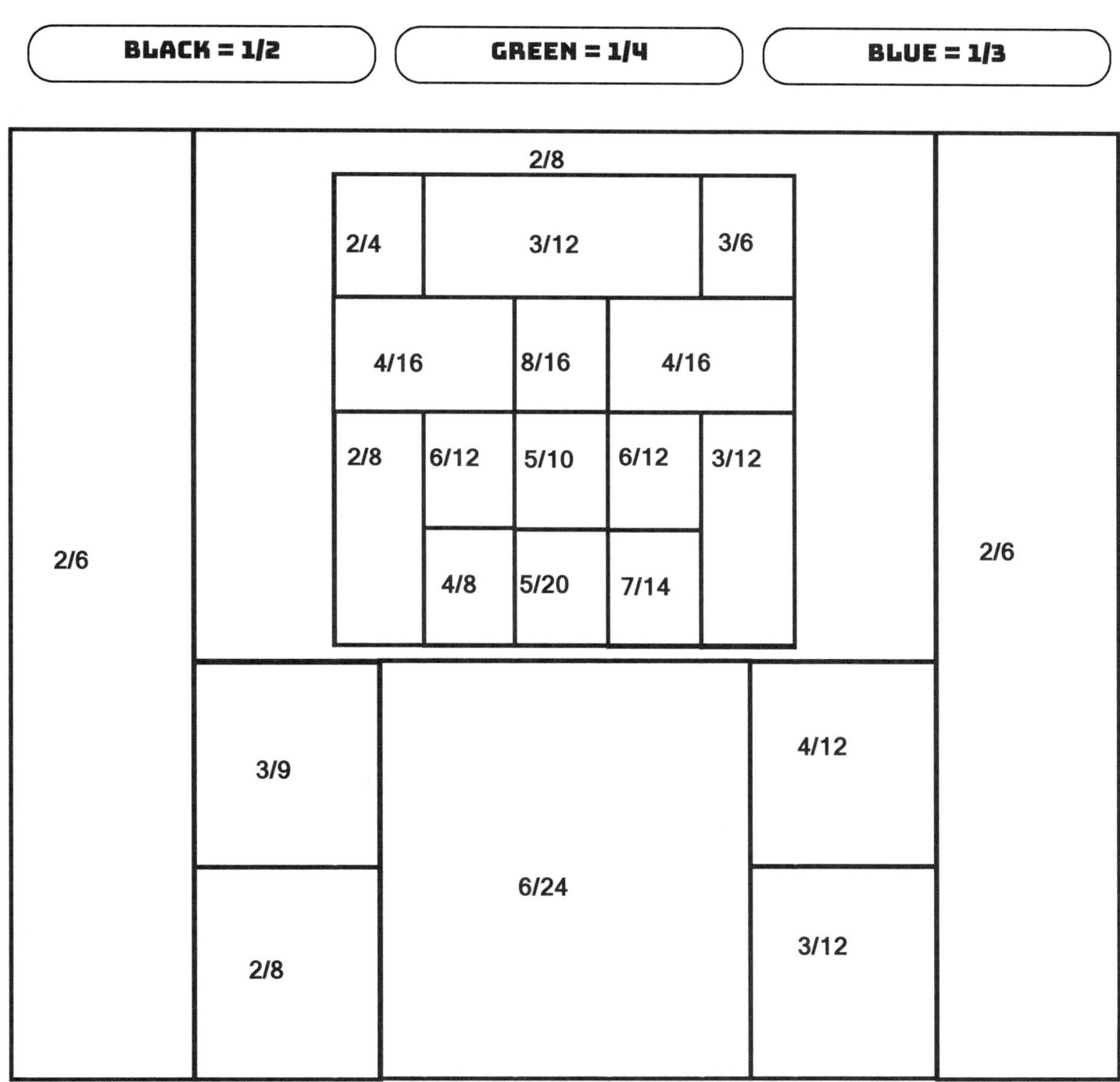

39

MINECRAFT DICE

There are no dice in Minecraft, but at times players might feel like they could use some. Below is a basic layout for a plain die. You can cut this out, using the outside lines to know where to cut, and fold it on the inside lines to make a cube. Once the cube is made, you can put numbers on it to use as a normal die, you can color in some of the squares certain colors to help you choose which blocks to use to build when you are playing Minecraft, or you can color the cube like a Minecraft block and make a bunch of them to build things in real life! The possibilities are endless!

Use the cut-out below to make your own die. You can also trace this pattern on other sheets of paper to make as many dice or Minecraft cubes as you want. Build with them, use them when you can't find a real die, or make up your own games to play with friends!

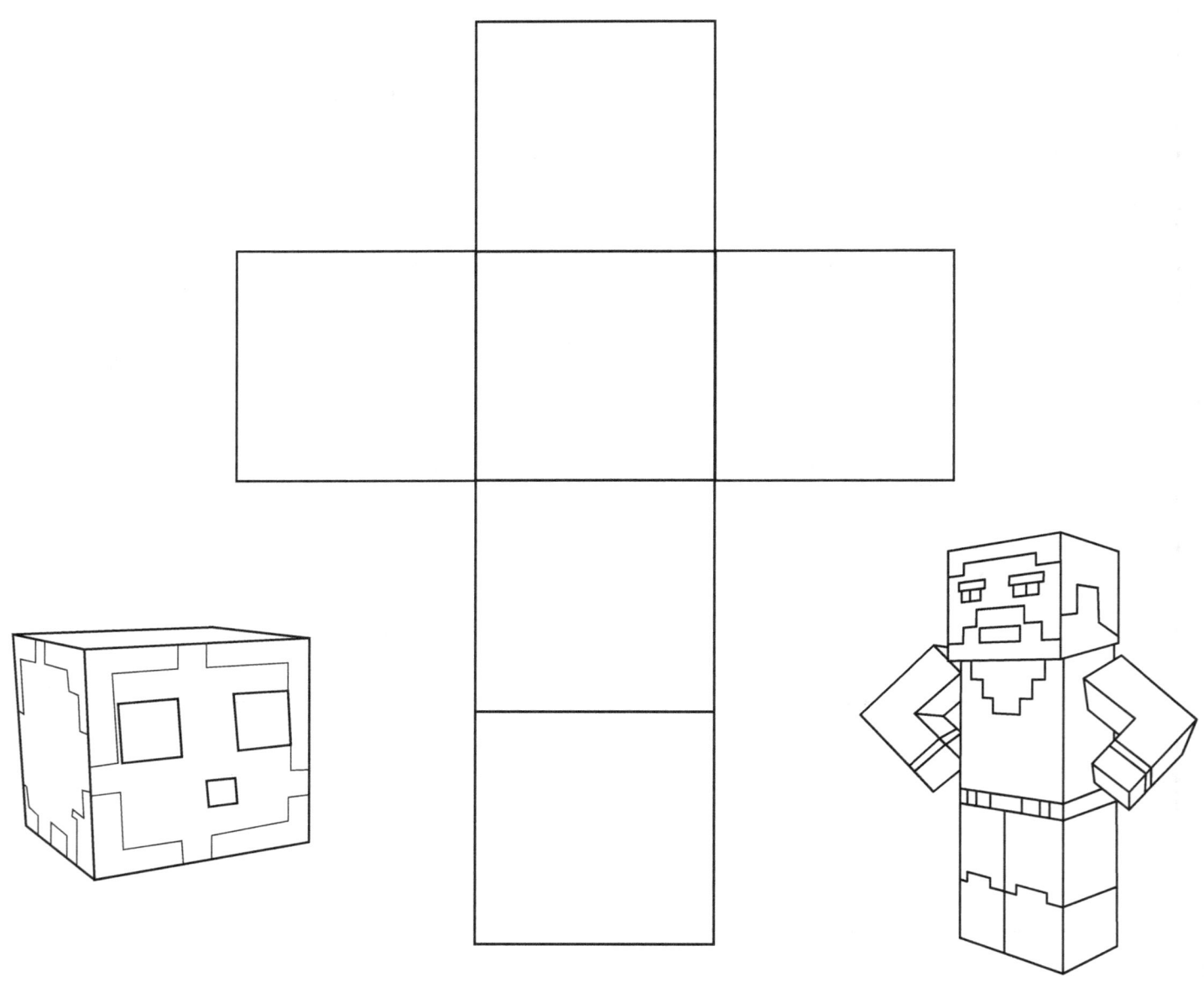

SCIENCE

UNSCRAMBLE THESE ACTIVITY NAMES

There are dozens of things to do in Minecraft, so many that all the fun activities could fill up a whole book. So, just see if you can unscramble these ten activity names you can do in Minecraft.

KOOINGC

FIHTGNIG

CAFTRNIG

GNISHFI

POTNOI WGNIRBE

XPOLRNIGE

RFMNAIG

ARGDNGEIN

NIMING

BUIDINGL

HINT: ALL OF THE WORDS END IN -ING

 # BIOME QUIZ

Do you think you know your biomes? This quiz will put your skills to the test! Below, there are descriptions of the biomes, and you must match them up with the right biome. When you are done with the quiz, you can grade yourself by using the answer sheet in the back of the book.

1. This biome is covered in snow. Not many trees grow here. If you are (un) lucky, you might even find a polar bear here!	a. Taiga b. Plains c. Ice Plains d. Frozen Ocean
2. This biome is sandy as can be. Cacti grow naturally here, but not much else does. It can be hard to find mobs here during the day because it is so bright and warm.	a. Savanna b. The Nether c. Beach d. Desert
3. This biome has both water and land. The water is darker than water in other biomes, and lily pads can be found here. Vines and sugarcane can be collected here, and mushrooms seem to be everywhere!	a. Forest b. Swampland c. River d. Hills
4. This biome is filled with wildlife and plants. Trees, flowers, and grass grow easily here. Many mobs can be found wandering around during the day. This is a great place to collect useful materials for crafting.	a. Desert b. Mesa c. Forest d. Plains
5. This biome's main feature is water, and it's everywhere. All the land in this area is under the water. Creatures can live in this water, but human characters will need a boat to get anywhere.	a. River b. Ocean c. The End d. Mushroom Island

UNSCRAMBLE THESE BIOME NAMES

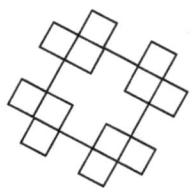

There are many different biomes to explore in the Overworld. Try to see if you can unscramble the names of a few of them!

CEI

SNALIP

GITAA

IHLLS

ESTORF

UNLGJE

CHABE

ESETRD

CAENO

VAANNAS

GUESS THE BIOME

The game is simple. There are 20 clues below. All you need to do is figure out what biome the clues are pointing to. If you think you have the answer before you get through all 20 clues, then you can check the answer pages to see if you got it right. If you are wrong, try to challenge someone else to this game to see if they can get it right.

1. Part of this area is flat and dry.
2. The other part is drooping and wet.
3. I have small pools filled with greenish water.
4. Lily pads are a common plant in the water.
5. The water is shallow, so it won't be hard to swim to the bottom.
6. At the bottom there is clay.
7. There is also sand at the bottom of the water.
8. Vines are everywhere here.
9. Mushrooms can be found here.
10. Sugarcane is the tastiest thing here.
11. Witches like to make their homes here.
12. Slimes sometimes like to pay a visit here.
13. This is a dangerous place to be at night.
14. Weather changes wildly here.
15. It does not usually snow here.
16. It does rain here.
17. The sky is gray here in the winter.
18. Sometimes the grass here is green, and sometimes it is yellow.
19. Depending on which place like this you visit, you will find different plants.
20. There are trees here.

CAN YOU GUESS WHAT BIOME THIS IS?

WHAT DO I EAT?

In Minecraft, most of the mobs don't eat other animals, with the exceptions being wolves, ocelots, and humans/villagers. In real life, many animals eat other animals, while some only eat plants.

HERBIVORES are creatures who don't eat meat, not even bugs! These creatures live off of plants only!

OMNIVORES eat both plants and animals. People are omnivores, since a healthy diet includes meat as well as vegetables and fruits.

CARNIVORES only eat meat. These creatures need to eat other animals to survive. It's not that they are too picky to get plants, it's just that they don't.

Here is a list of mobs in Minecraft. Write down whether you think they are herbivores, omnivores, or carnivores under the headings below. When you are done, you can check your answers in the back of the book.

MOBS: Cow, Chicken, Horse, Wolf, Ocelot, Pig, Human, Villager, and Sheep.

HERBIVORE	OMNIVORE	CARNIVORE

 # MAMMAL OR NOT?

There are many mobs in Minecraft, and there are many different ways to put them into categories. One of the ways to categorize mobs is to know if they are mammals or not.

MAMMALS are warm-blooded creatures with vertebrae (spines). Mammals have hair on their bodies. Mother mammals can feed their babies with milk. Mammals do not lay eggs. Some mammals, like whales and dolphins, can live underwater.

Below is a list of animal mobs in Minecraft. Try to figure out if they are mammals or not.

Horse, Cow, Pig, Squid, Silverfish, Sheep, Bat, Spider, Chicken, Wolf, Ocelot.

MAMMAL	NOT MAMMAL

SCIENCE WORD SEARCH

There are dozens of kinds of sciences that are shown in the real world, and in Minecraft. Try to see if you can find these ten science words in this word search.

WORDS: Anatomy, Astronomy, Biology, Chemistry, Ecology, Geology, Neuroscience, Oceanography, Physics, and Science.

```
Y W N Q B K L E E W V O Y P M
D M B S L I C C S H C G R H J
O C O E E N O V O E H I T Y X
Y J W N E L K L A F P Y S S W
D G D I O G I N O Q K M I I V
Y F C G Z R O T D G U W M C H
B S Y T G G T V U V Y O E S M
I C N T R M D S Z L Z V H K A
Z Y D A Y M O T A N A X C M J
I F P E C N E I C S O R U E N
K H L W G E O L O G Y S S J T
Y C R I N I S G Z L B J J K C
R L K Q U D F O C H Z U X P E
J F X R U L V I V N I S E G Y
W W U W U J P N R M M L P C W
```

48

STONE WORDSEARCH

There are many basic stones in Minecraft that make it the wonderful world players know and love. Below is a wordsearch with ten different stone names in it. Do you think you can solve this puzzle? Good luck!

WORDS TO FIND:

- ANDESITE
- BEDROCK
- CLAY
- DIORITE
- ENDSTONE
- GRANITE
- SANDSTONE
- QUARTZ
- OBSIDIAN
- PRISMARINE

```
g c u p c y k n h e q l t c w
b j i i i n a u n q u a r t z
g c b z o i r d y s c l a y o
q o s k d r s v v g t c e j k
b o q i m t o s t u f l o n u
s e s e o a n d e s i t e a d
l b d n n i k l e g f g z i g
o h e r c o p j n z m j o o v
j o t i o v t k p w j r x g t
k v j v a c n s e h i k n u l
y b x g k e k k d t s k j q r
y t q t s u t s e n x b m z y
e n i r a m s i r p a s n h b
i a w g e j o p n t j s l h m
e t i n a r g g n y f g m s l
```

WEATHER WORD SEARCH

There are many types of weather in Minecraft. Try to solve this weather word search and see if you can find the nine weather words listed below. Good luck!

WORDS: Blizzard, cloudy, lightning, overcast, rain, snow, sunny, thunder, and windy.

```
U M R P V T B B O I B X U L M
Q Y L N S G C C P I E K Q X W
X I Z B N H V H V S T H W N R
T A T H E A D H D N V T V R P
S I G N I N T H G I L S D R L
M X F O W Q M W Q T G A N I Y
D A M R N U S V X R X C N I O
Z R N Z X E N U A J Z R P K O
Y H A A Z G Z I N E W E Q Z R
C N U Z W O N S I N W V K E W
W Z H U Z C L O U D Y O D S V
I D L O G I F P E J D N I X N
N Z C C V O L G A Z U Q L M Q
D M N K P V I B Z H L T E N P
Y F G J I M L D T E Z G C O L
```

HOW TO MAKE COOL FIREWORKS

In Minecraft, there are a few different types of fireworks you can make, and some are cooler to look at than others. Below are some basic instructions on how to make some of the coolest types of firework stars. Try this out next time you play the game.

For all fireworks, a 3x3 crafting grid is needed. All fireworks need a firework star, paper, and gunpowder to explode. A firework rocket can be made with only paper and gunpowder, but this will not have a cool explosion effect.

PURPLE CREEPER FIREWORK STAR

Gunpowder	Magenta Dye	
	Creeper Head	

GREEN TWINKLE FIREWORK STAR

Gunpowder	Cactus Green	
Feather	Glowstone Dust	

STAR-SHAPED BLUE FIREWORK STAR

Gunpowder	Lapis Lazuli	
Gold Nugget	Diamond	

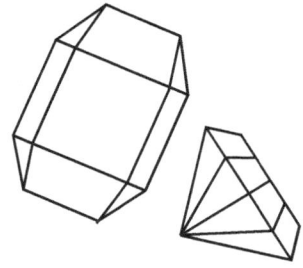

HOW TO TAME ANIMALS

It's easy to find a stray cow or pig to bring onto a farm, but it can be tricky to find a wolf or ocelot to make your pet. Luckily, this activity book has instructions on how to do just that, and it is easier than it sounds. All you need to do is collect some supplies, have some good luck, and have some fun to make this work.

TAMING WOLVES:

To tame a wolf you will need bones. You can collect these by fighting skeletons. There is no telling for sure how many bones it will take to tame a wolf. Each bone has a 1/3 chance of taming a wolf, so you should have a little more than three bones, to be safe.

Throw a bone at the wolf to let them eat it. When the wolf is tamed, little hearts will appear around its head and it will get a collar. Once this happens, you don't need to feed it bones anymore. You can click on the wolf to name it, give it commands, and have it follow you around.

TAMING OCELOTS:

To tame an ocelot you will need fish. You can get these by fishing. Like wolves, just one fish is not guaranteed to tame an ocelot, so you will need a few to make sure you have enough to tame the ocelot.

Throw fish at the ocelot until little hearts appear around its head. When this happens, it is tamed and you can name it.

MAKING A LEASH:

If you want to lead your furry friend around with you, you can use a leash. All you need to make it are four pieces of string and a slimeball. Arrange them like below and you can use the leash on your pet (and many other passive mobs). Have fun!

String	String	
String	Slimeball	String

HOW TO MAKE CAKE IN MINECRAFT AND REAL LIFE

Making a cake in Minecraft is a fun way to use up some extra materials your character can get from farming and taking care of animals. To make a cake in the game, you will need these things:

- 3x3 crafting grid area
- 3 milk
- 3 wheat
- 2 sugar
- 1 egg

To make the cake, you will need to put the ingredients in the grid in this exact order. If you put them in any other order, the recipe won't work.

Milk	Milk	Milk
Sugar	Egg	Sugar
Wheat	Wheat	Wheat

Once you do this, you will have a Minecraft cake or cupcakes of your own! This recipe is very close to an actual cake recipe that you can make with help from a parent or guardian. To make a Minecraft inspired cake, you will need these things:

Once you do this, you will have a Minecraft cake or cupcakes of your own! This recipe is very close to an actual cake recipe that you can make with help from a parent or guardian. To make a Minecraft inspired cake, you will need these things:

- Oven
- Cake pan or nonstick muffin tin
- 2 Mixing bowls
- Measuring cups
- Mixing spoons, whisks, or a rubber spatula
- 1 1/2 cups flour
- 1 cup sugar
- 1/2 cup milk
- 1/2 cup butter
- 2 teaspoons baking powder
- 2 teaspoons vanilla extract
- One container of your favorite frosting
- Sprinkles (optional)

Many of these ingredients are similar to the ones used for the Minecraft cake, so when this is done, you will get to taste what your characters are eating! Follow these instructions with help from a parent or guardian to make the cake.

1. Preheat the oven to 350
2. Mix all the flour, sugar, and baking soda in one bowl
3. Melt the butter in the microwave on high for about 30 seconds
4. Put the melted butter, milk, and vanilla extract into the other mixing bowl and mix
5. Slowly mix the wet ingredients into the dry ingredients until the batter is smooth
6. Put the cake batter into the cake pan or muffin tin and into the oven
7. Bake the cake for 30 minutes or until done
8. Let the cake or cupcakes cool completely and then put on the frosting and sprinkles

ENJOY!

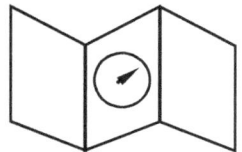 # MAKE YOUR OWN MAP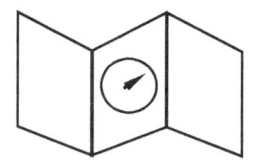

All you need in Minecraft to make a map is eight pieces of paper and a compass arranged in a 3x3 crafting area. These maps are simple to make and let you see where you are going in Minecraft.

Paper	Paper	Paper
Paper	Compass	Paper
Paper	Paper	Paper

Making your own map of a fantasy world outside of Minecraft can be way more fun. All you need to do it are these four things:

1. Paper
2. Pencil (with an eraser)
3. Colored Pencils, crayons, or markers
4. Cereal or dry macaroni noodles

Once you have these things, it can be easy and fun to make a map of your own. Follow these easy steps to make your own map.

1. Put the paper on a flat surface, like a table.
2. Take a small handful of cereal or noodles and gently drop them on the paper.
3. Trace the outline of the food. This will make an island map. There may even be small islands outside of it!
4. Clean up the food.
5. Color in the map however you want! You can use blue crayons to draw in rivers or lakes, green to make plains and forests, brown to make sandy deserts, and white to make snowy places. You can even draw little triangles or points to make mountain ranges.

You can do this over and over again to make different shaped maps, and you can color them differently to make it look like they have different biomes, just like in Minecraft.

TRY IT NOW!

MAKE YOUR OWN SLIME

Slime can make things sticky in Minecraft, but it can be sticky and fun in real life! By trying this experiment, you can make your own slime! It won't connect to pistons well like it does in Minecraft, but it will be fun to play with!

All you need to do this experiment are these things: mixing bowl, plastic bag, food coloring (optional), 1/4 cup water, 1/4 cup liquid glue, and 1/4 cup liquid starch (ask an adult for this).

Once you have the items above, all you have to do is follow these instructions to make your own slime.

1. Put all the water and glue into the bowl and stir it together.
2. Add the food coloring now if you want it. If you don't use it, the slime will be white.
3. Add the liquid starch and stir some more.
4. Put the mixture in a plastic bag.
5. While still in the bag, try to move the slime with your hands. Do this until it feels almost like molding clay, but softer.
6. Once the slime is mixed, you can play with it inside or outside of the bag.
7. When you are done playing, put the slime back in the bag so it doesn't dry out.

HAVE FUN WITH YOUR SLIME!

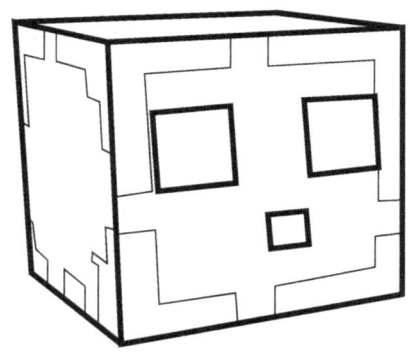

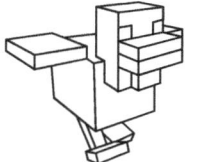
NATURE BINGO

Minecraft is full of plants and animals, and so is the great outdoors! Go outside with an adult or their permission and try to find enough things on this list to get a bingo (five in a row across, down, or diagonal). You can make your own or a copy of this one to challenge a friend!

You do not need to pick up the things you find, just color in the square when you see the thing on the bingo sheet.

B	I	N	G	O
GRASS	BROWN ROCK	SPIDER	ACORN	BLUE FLOWER
SAND	PUDDLE	SPARKLY ROCK	ANT	MUD
GREEN LEAF	BUTTERFLY	FREE SPACE	SNOW	LADYBUG
BIRD	SQUIRREL	FROG	BROWN LEAF	YELLOW FLOWER
TADPOLE	STICK	BUMBLE BEE	RABBIT	BIRD'S NEST

TECHNOLOGY

DECODE THE SECRET MESSAGE

Steve has been sent a secret message for one of his missions, and he needs your help to solve it! Below is a secret code you can use to decode the secret message below. Solve the puzzle to help out Steve!

A = △ B = ▽ C = ∇ D = ⱱ E = ✝ F = ⚲

G = ⚵ H = ≋ I = ⊖ J = ① K = ⊕ L = ⊘

M = ४ N = ◇ O = ♂ P = ⊕ Q = ☺ R = ♛

S = ⌒ T = ⊤ U = ⚲ V = ⚴ W = ⚘ X = ✳

Y = ⊼ Z = ₩

G O   T O   T H E   C A V E   T O   D E F E A T   T H E   E N C H A N T E R

E N D E R D R A G O N

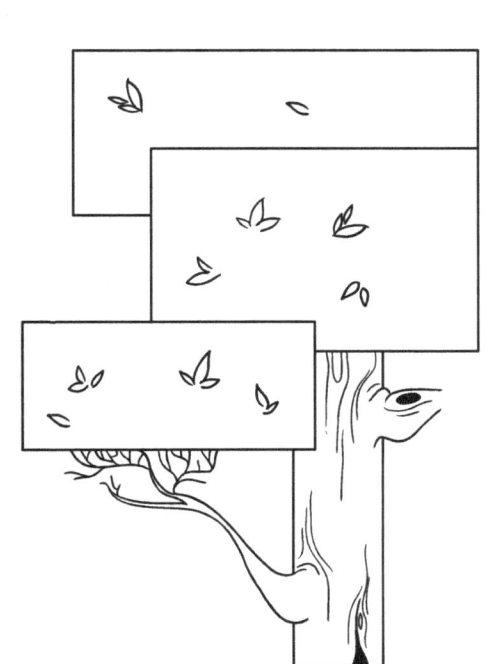
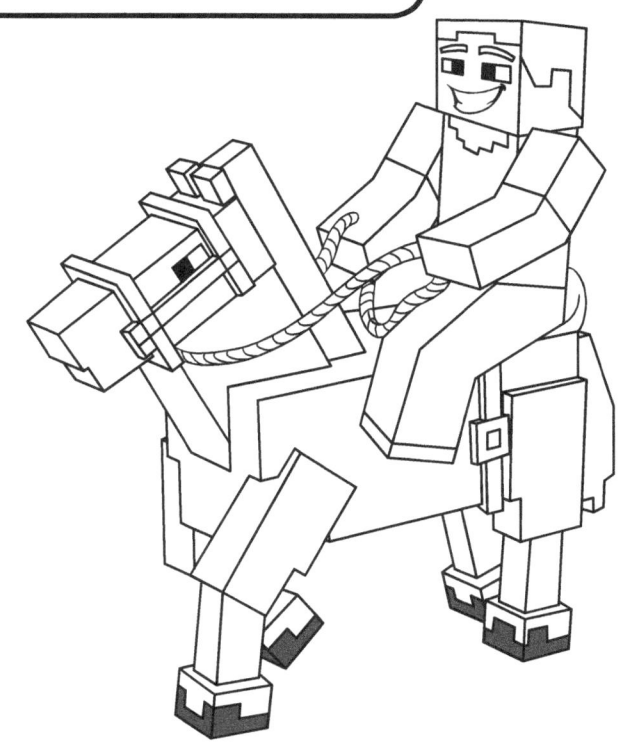

SOLVE THE MAZE!

Solve this maze by starting on the left side and working your way to the exit on the right.

Use a pencil so you can erase your line if you make a mistake.

HINT: If you get stuck, try starting a new line from the exit end of the maze and connecting it to the one you started from the entrance to the maze.

PROBLEM SOLVING WITH TNT

Mining can be a fun and challenging way to collect all sorts of different materials when you are not on creative mode in Minecraft. Sometimes using TNT is a great way to get what you need, but other times, tools like pickaxes and shovels can get the job done better.

In case you don't already know, this is how you make a block of TNT. All you need is gunpowder and sand (or red sand). Put the materials into a 3x3 crafting area as shown below and you are sure to get an explosive block of TNT.

Gunpowder	(Red) Sand	Gunpowder
(Red) Sand	Gunpowder	(Red) Sand
Gunpowder	(Red) Sand	Gunpowder

Once you have the TNT, all you need to do to make it work is set it on fire (and back away before it explodes). You can do this with a torch, with an enchanted flaming arrow, by exploding a nearby Creeper, or even by exploding another block of TNT.

Below is a list of experiments you can try in Minecraft to find out if TNT or smaller, less explosive tools, will be better for the job. You can do these experiments as often as you want. You can write your results on the lines below, or use a separate piece of paper.

1. Try to start a mine in the side of a mountain. Which tool makes a mine faster?

a. _____

2. Go to a mine you have used before. Once inside the mine, use TNT once to see what happens. Does this get you more or less materials than when you use smaller tools?

a. _____

3. For non-mining uses, try both small tools and TNT to fight any mobs that try to attack. Which works better for winning the fight?

a. _____

ONCE YOU HAVE ALL THESE QUESTIONS ANSWERED, YOU CAN USE YOUR FINDINGS TO SOLVE FUTURE PROBLEMS IN MINECRAFT!

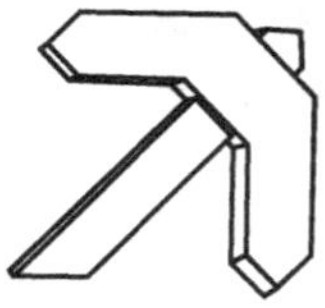

A MAZE AND A SHOVEL

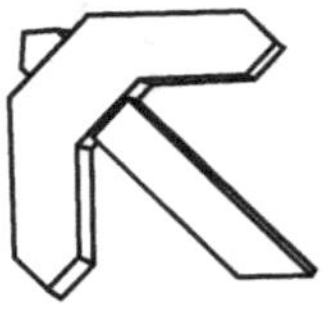

Whether you are doing a maze on paper or going through one in Minecraft, getting through a maze can be tricky. Some people might want to cheat or give up when things get tough, but there's a better way to go about solving a maze.

When you are doing a maze on paper, using a pencil is a great idea. That way, if you mess up, you can just erase your mistakes and try again. Try it here with this maze.

When going through a maze in Minecraft, you can't use a pencil, but you can use a shovel. Don't just hack down whatever is in your way to get through the maze, because that's cheating. Instead, shovel up the ground you walk on. This will make a path, that way you will know if you have been somewhere before or not. This easy trick can save you a lot of time in Minecraft. Try this trick next time you play the game!

SOUNDS LIKE...A PUZZLE

There are many types of ores that can be used to craft things in Minecraft. Below is a list of ore names - well, words that sounds like ore names, anyway. Can you guess which sound-alike word matches up with each type of ore? Check your answers in the back of the book when you are done to see if you got them all right!

HINT: If you get stuck, try using rhyming words or saying the word out loud to figure out what it could be. Remember that all of these are types of ores.

1. GOAL	
2. EYE EARN	
3. ALMOND	
4. LAP IS LAZY E	
5. M. ROUND	
6. BED TONE	
7. COLD	

THE RIGHT TOOL FOR THE JOB

As all experienced Minecraft players know, there are many tools in Minecraft, all of which do different jobs. Below is a quiz to test your Minecraft tool skills. Match the job being done with the best tool to do it. Some jobs can be done with more than one tool, but you need to pick the tool that does the best work for each job. When you are done, you can check your answers in the back of the book.

1. The best tool for tilling a garden is...

    a. Shears

    b. Flint

    c. Pickaxe

    d. Hoe

2. The best tool for digging through tough rock is...

    a. Shovel

    b. Axe

    c. Pickaxe

    d. Steel

3. The best tool for digging through soft rock is..

    a. Bucket

    b. Compass

    c. Shovel

    d. Hoe

4. The best tool for catching dinner is...

    a. Bucket

    b. Fishing Rod

    c. Shovel

    d. Pickaxe

5. The best tool for finding your way when you are lost is...

    a. Hoe

    b. Steel

    c. Clock

    d. Compass

HOW TO MAKE A ROLLER COASTER WITH REDSTONE

Making railroads in Minecraft can be fun, but making roller coasters can be even more fun. It's as easy as making a railroad, but can make a minecart move faster along the rails, go up or down hills, and generally just be more complicated (but more fun) to make.

All you need to make a roller coaster is some rails, powered rails, redstone, minecart, piston, and a hilly area (or blocks to make a hill out of). This is most easily done on creative mode, but it is still possible to make all the parts on other modes of the game.

Follow these instructions to make your very own roller coaster.

1. Find a hilly area to make your roller coaster, or build hills and trenches for your roller coaster rails to go on.

2. Place the rails where you want your roller coaster to go. It can be as long or short as you want it to be.

3. If your rails are going uphill, replace the normal rails with power rails. You can also put power rails in places where you want the minecart to go faster. It is also a good idea to put one or two power rails at the beginning of the tracks.

4. Put redstone on the side of the power rails. This will help to power them.

5. Place a piston before the starting point of the roller coaster. This will push the minecart to start the roller coaster ride.

6. Place the minecart at the beginning of the tracks.

7. Get in the minecart and enjoy the ride!

YOU CAN DO THIS AS MANY TIMES AS YOU WANT TO MAKE DIFFERENT TRACKS. EXPERIMENT WITH THESE INSTRUCTIONS TO MAKE THE BEST TRACK YOU CAN!

 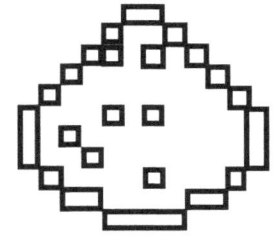

HOW TO MAKE YOUR OWN PUZZLE

Building puzzles can be fun, but making puzzles can be even more fun because you get to make the design. Making a puzzle isn't hard, either. All you have to do it make a drawing, cut it out, cut the puzzle piece shapes, and then put it back together again.

Start by drawing your puzzle in the square below. You can draw whatever you want, as long as it fits in the square.

When you are done drawing your picture, cut out the square along the black lines.

Once your picture is cut out, cut it into puzzle piece shapes. You might want to draw the shapes on the back of the picture before you do this so you know where to cut, but you don't have to.

WHEN YOU ARE DONE CUTTING, CHALLENGE YOUR FRIENDS TO TRY YOUR NEW PUZZLE. SINCE THIS IS SO EASY, YOU CAN DO THIS AS OFTEN AS YOU WANT WITH SOME OF YOUR OTHER DRAWINGS. HAVE FUN!

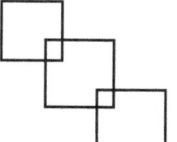 # MINECRAFT PAPER BLOCKS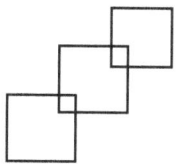

Building things in Minecraft can be fun, but sometimes staring at a computer or TV for too long can make your eyes hurt. A great way to still make things and to rest your eyes at the same time is to make your own paper Minecraft blocks.

All you have to do to make your own paper blocks is color the blocks to make them look like the blocks you want to use, and then cut them out. You can start with the block chart on this page, and then make more on other pieces of paper as you need them.

If you get help from a parent or guardian, you can also glue these blocks onto thin sheets of magnets and cut them out so you can stick them to doors, refrigerators, and any other magnetic surface to show your pictures there.

Also, if you like the designs you make, you can paste them on a piece of paper so you can keep them for as long as you want. Try to make some blocks now and see what you can make outside of Minecraft!

 # RESOURCE MANAGEMENT PERSONALITY QUIZ

Do you handle your resources well? Take this personality quiz to find out if you are a resource management genius, if you are average at resource management, or if you could stand to learn a thing or two about it.

1. What do you do during the day in Minecraft?

   a. Hunt
   b. Explore
   c. Build things

2. What do you do at night in Minecraft?

   a. Build things
   b. Explore
   c. Hunt

3. You see a cow in the game. What do you do?

   a. Bring it to your home
   b. Kill it
   c. Milk it

4. A zombie is coming! What do you do?

   a. Fight with a sword
   b. Fight with a bow and arrow
   c. Run away

5. Where do you build your houses most of the time?

   a. In the side of a mountain/cave
   b. In the forest
   c. In a clearing

Check your answers and use the chart to find out your score

MOSTLY A'S	MOSTLY B'S	MOSTLY C'S
You are a resource management genius!	You are average at resource management.	You could learn a thing or two about resource management.

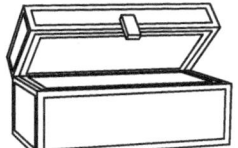

TOOL STORY

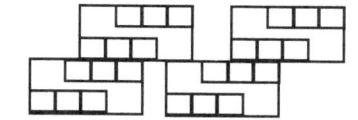

Tools are an important part to any Minecraft story, but have you ever tried to make your own story? Write a small story below that uses at least four of the tool words below. It doesn't matter how long the story is, just as long as you have fun writing it! You can use more pieces of paper if you need to. For an extra challenge, you can also try to use more than four of the words below.

PICKAXE, SHOVEL, SHEARS, INGOT, FISHING, CLOCK, COMPASS, LEAD, VILLAGER, FARM, MINE, TNT, FURNACE, CHEST, CRAFTING.

ANSWER KEY

Pg- 44
Unscramble These Biome Names

1. Ice
2. Plains
3. Taiga
4. Hills
5. Forest
6. Jungle
7. Beach
8. Desert
9. Ocean
10. Savanna

Pg-22
Flower Shop Math

a. 1. 5
b. 2. 20
c. 3. 5
d. 4. 30
e. 12

Pg-32
Steve's Odd Party

1. B
2. A
3. B
4. A
5. C

Pg-28
Mineral Math

1. 12
2. 3
3. 2
4. No. You would need 4 more gold
   blocks.
5. You will have 2 left over.

Pg-43
Biome Quiz

1. C
2. D
3. B
4. C
5. B

Pg-14
Match the Tools

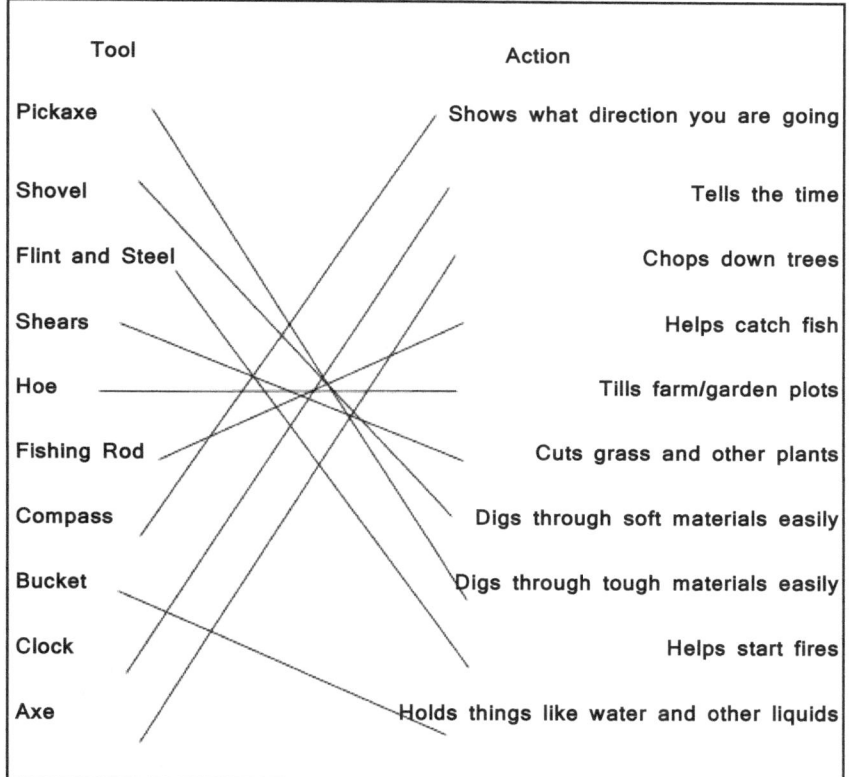

Pg- 21 Farming Math Brain Teasers	Pg- 64 The Right Tool for the Job
1. Yes, 3. 2. 90, no (she only needs 9) 3. 3	1. D 2. C 3. C 4. B 5. D
Pg- 24 How Many Blocks...	Pg- 59 Decode the Secret Message
1. 30, 20 2. 35, 70, 210	Go to the cave to defeat the escaped Enderdragon

Pg- 42 **Unscramble These Activity Names** 1. Cooking 2. Fighting 3. Crafting 4. Fishing 5. Potion Brewing 6. Exploring 7. Farming 8. Gardening 9. Mining 10. Building	**Pg- 27** **Math Message** 1. To Alex 2. I am coming to visit you for your birthday 3. I will bring cake 4. I hope you like it 5. From Steve
Pg- 47 **Mammal or Not?** Mammal: Horse, Cow, Pig, Sheep, Bats, Wolf, Ocelot Not Mammal: Squid, Silverfish, Spider, Chicken	**Pg- 20** **Family Photo** There are 8 people in the photo. 4 kids, their parents, and their grandparents.

Pg- 63 Sounds Like...A Puzzle 1. Coal 2. Iron 3. Diamond 4. Lapis Lazuli 5. Emrald 6. Redstone 7. Gold	**Pg- 23** Guess the Mob Math 1. 20 health points 2. 49 attack strength 3. 7 light level 4. 5 experience points 5. 1 lightning bolt 6. I am a Creeper
Pg- 46 What Do I Eat? Herbivores: Cow, Chicken, Horse, Pig, Sheep Omnivores: Human, Villager Carnivores: Wolf, Ocelot	**Pg- 31** Square Numbers in Math 1. 1 2. 4 3. 9 4. 16 5. 25 6. 36 7. 49 8. 64 9. 81 10. 100

Pg- 30
Pigs in a Pen

Pg- 20
Sudoku

8	1	4	7	6	3	2	9	5
5	2	9	4	1	8	7	3	6
6	3	7	2	5	9	8	1	4
7	9	3	8	2	6	5	4	1
2	5	6	1	7	4	9	8	3
4	8	1	9	3	5	6	2	7
1	4	2	6	8	7	3	5	9
9	7	5	3	4	2	1	6	8
3	6	8	5	9	1	4	7	2

Pg- 25
Make Four

1. 3
2. 2
3. 1
4. 1
5. 1
6. 2
7. 3
8. 2
9. 5
10. 6

Pg- 29

Name Game

Name/Mob	Even	Odd
Steve		✓
Alex	✓	
Blaze		✓
Creeper		✓
Enderman	✓	
Ghast		✓
Iron Golem		✓
Villager	✓	
Zombie	✓	
Snow Golem		✓

Pg- 34 **Telling Time** 1. 20 minutes 2. 3 3. 8:00pm 4. a. 3 days. b. 3 nights. 5. 4	**Pg-45** **Guess the Biome** This is the Swampland biome.
Pg- 19 **Count by...** 1. 8, 12 2. 15, 30 3. 30, 70 4. 9, 15 5. 8, 16 6. 18, 36 7. 50, 100 8. 300, 500 9. 6, 10.5 10. 3/2 (or 1 1/2), 2 (or 4/2)	**Pg-26** **Math Brain Teasers** 1. They both weigh the same 2. He has five sheep 3. Every month 4. Alex has three apples 5. 100% Hens are always girls, roosters are the boy chickens.

Pg-36
Tangram Cat

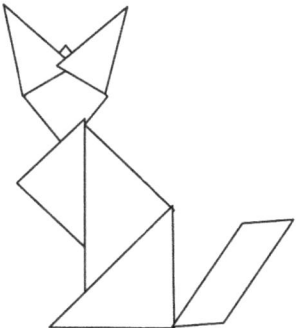

www.ingramcontent.com/pod-product-compliance
Lightning Source LLC
Chambersburg PA
CBHW081755100526
44592CB00015B/2442